Easy Piano
CARTOON TUNES 2nd Edition

ISBN-13: 978-0-7935-3044-1
ISBN-10: 0-7935-3044-X

HAL•LEONARD®
CORPORATION
7777 W. BLUEMOUND RD. P.O. BOX 13819 MILWAUKEE, WI 53213

Visit Hal Leonard Online at
www.halleonard.com

CONTENTS

BETTY BOOP
from the Paramount Cartoon

Words by EDWARD HEYMAN
Music by JOHN W. GREEN

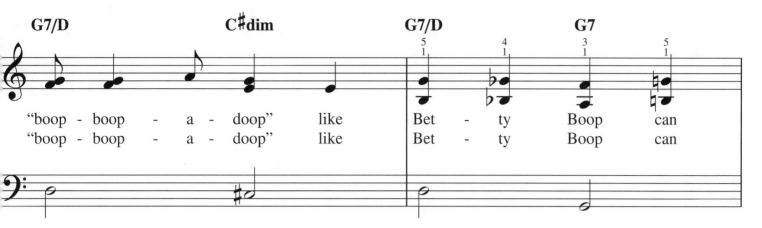

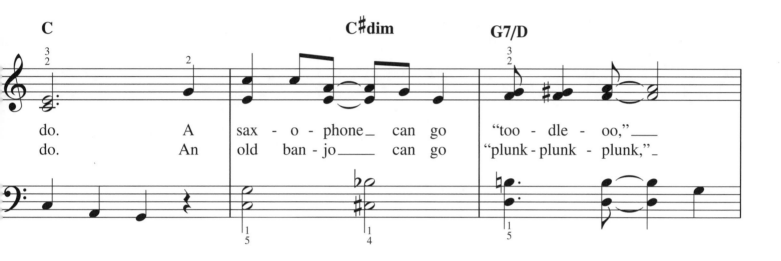

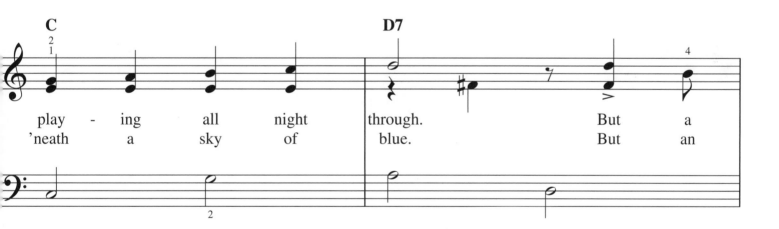

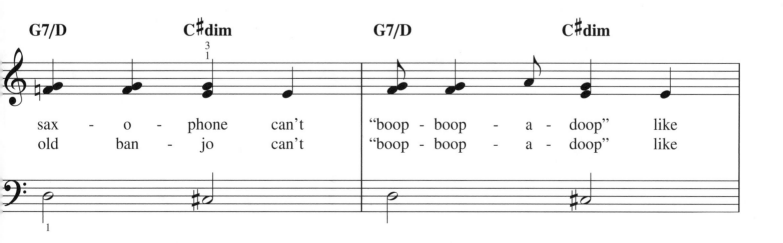

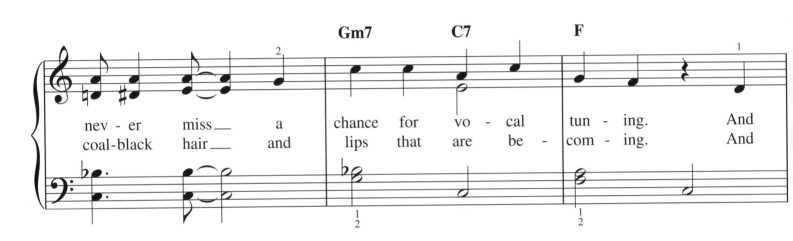

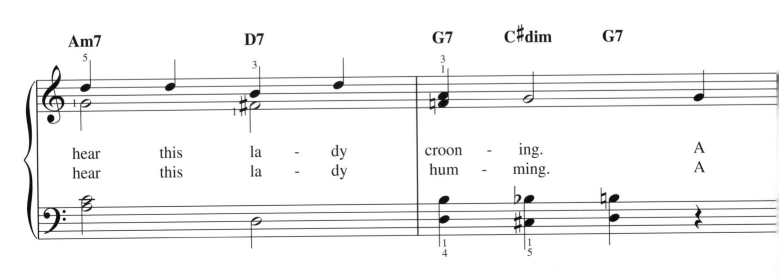

Additional Lyrics

3. A poodle dog can go "woof-woof-woof," Scotties do it, too.
But a poodle dog can't "boop-boop-a-doop" like Betty Boop can do.
A Jersey cow can go "moo-moo-moo," all the long day through.
But a Jersey cow can't "boop-boop-a-doop" like Betty Boop can do.

This gal has got a lot that's hot, she leaves a spell that's clinging.
And anytime and anywhere you can hear this lady singing.
An auto horn can go "beep-beep-beep," down the avenue.
But an auto horn can't "boop-boop-a-doop" like Betty Boop can do.

BOB THE BUILDER
"INTRO THEME SONG"

Words and Music by
PAUL JOYCE

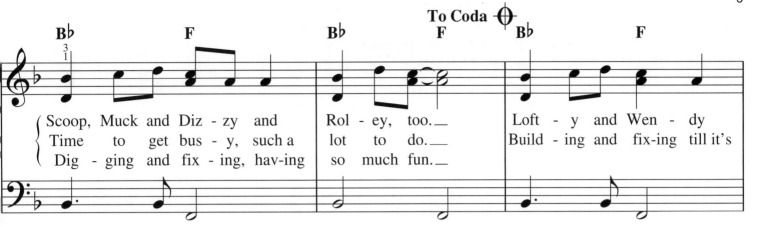

Scoop, Muck and Diz - zy and / Rol - ey, too. __ / Loft - y and Wen - dy
Time to get bus - y, such a / lot to do. __ / Build - ing and fix-ing till it's
Dig - ging and fix - ing, hav-ing / so much fun. __

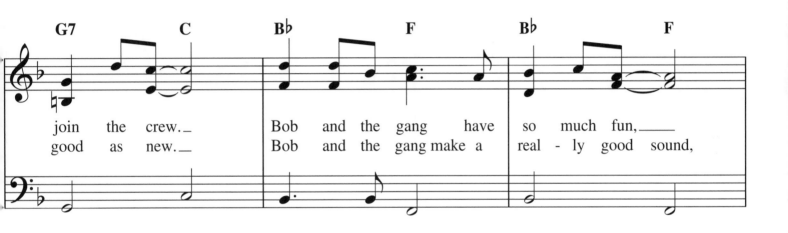

join the crew. __ / Bob and the gang have / so much fun, ____
good as new. __ / Bob and the gang make a / real - ly good sound,

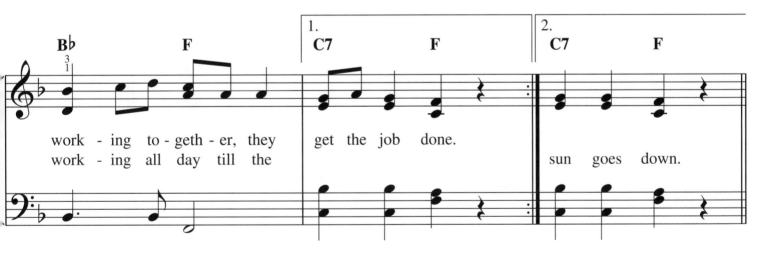

work - ing to-geth - er, they / get the job done.
work - ing all day till the / sun goes down.

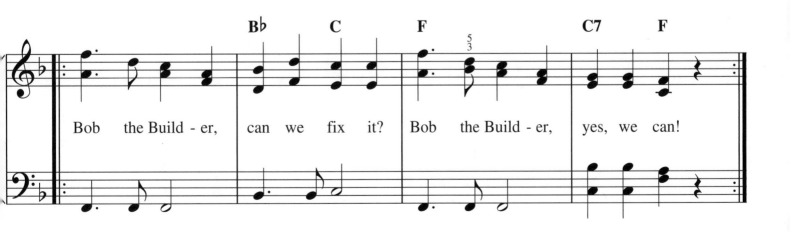

Bob the Build - er, can we fix it? Bob the Build - er, yes, we can!

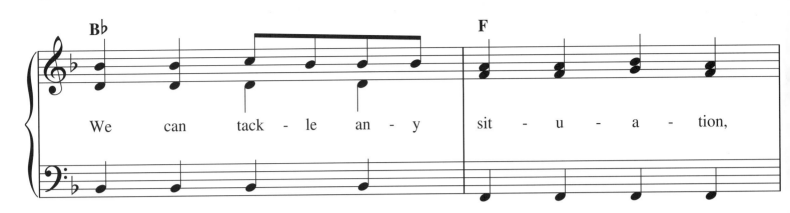

We can tack - le an - y sit - u - a - tion,

D.S. al Coda

look out, here we come!

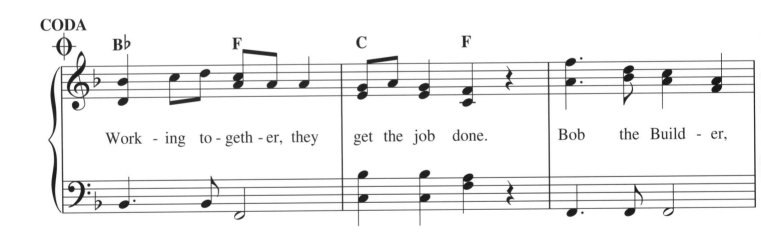

CODA

Work - ing to - geth - er, they get the job done. Bob the Build - er,

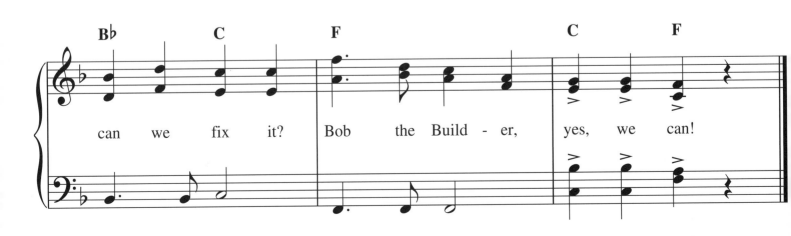

can we fix it? Bob the Build - er, yes, we can!

CASPER THE FRIENDLY GHOST

from the Paramount Cartoon

Words by MACK DAVID
Music by JERRY LIVINGSTON

C#dim

friend - ly ghost, he could-n't be bad or mean. He'll

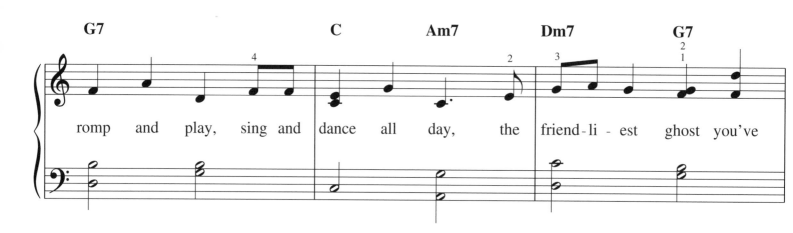

G7 **C** **Am7** **Dm7** **G7**

romp and play, sing and dance all day, the friend-li - est ghost you've

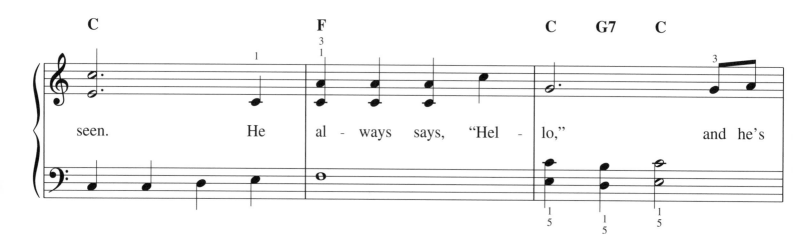

C **F** **C** **G7** **C**

seen. He al - ways says, "Hel - lo," and he's

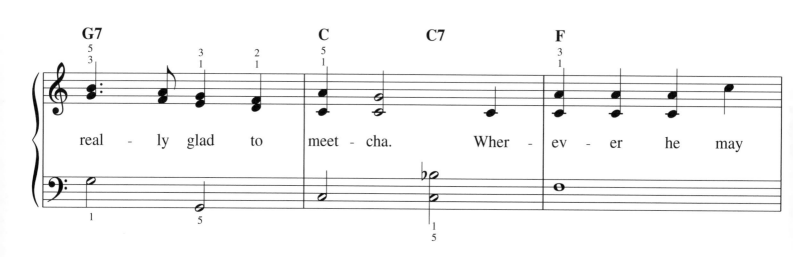

G7 **C** **C7** **F**

real - ly glad to meet - cha. Wher - ev - er he may

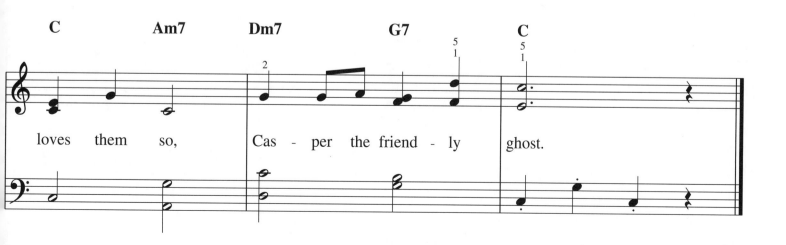

DORA THE EXPLORER THEME SONG

from DORA THE EXPLORER

Words and Music by JOSH SITRON,
BILLY STRAUS and SARAH DURKEE

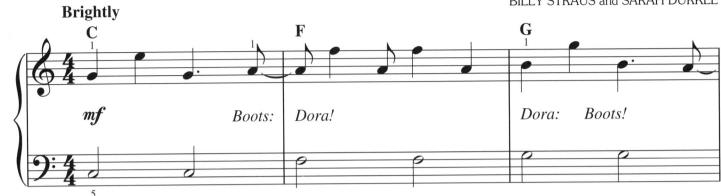

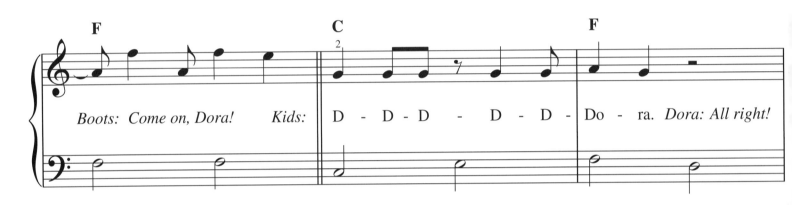

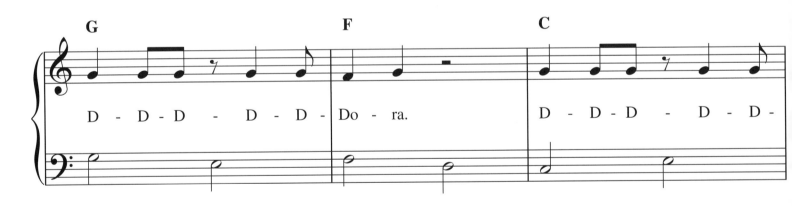

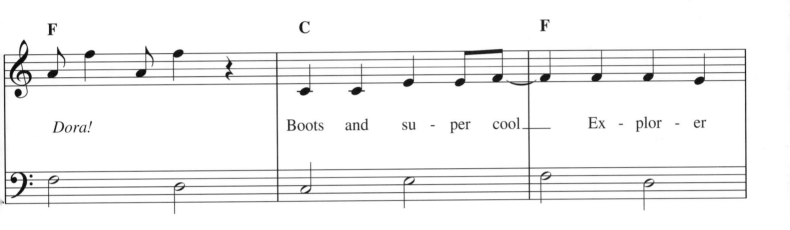

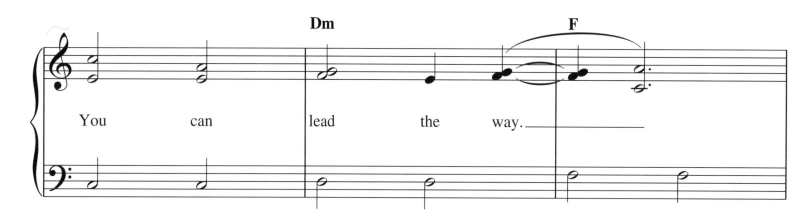

You can lead the way.

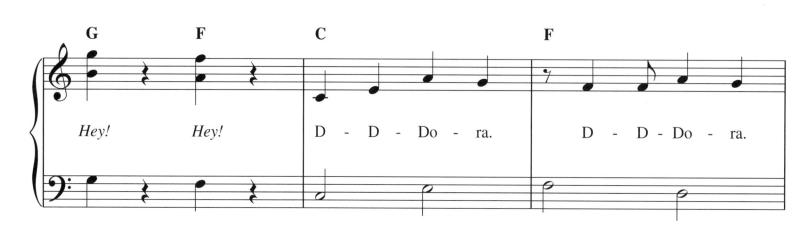

Hey! Hey! D - D - Do - ra. D - D - Do - ra.

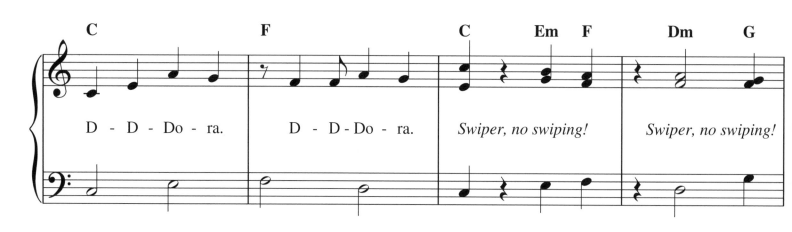

D - D - Do - ra. D - D - Do - ra. *Swiper, no swiping!* *Swiper, no swiping!*

Swiper: Oh, man! *Kids:* Do - ra the Ex - plor - er!

FELIX THE WONDERFUL CAT
from the Television Series

Words and Music by
WINSTON SHARPLES

nar - ry._____ He's the kind of guy that

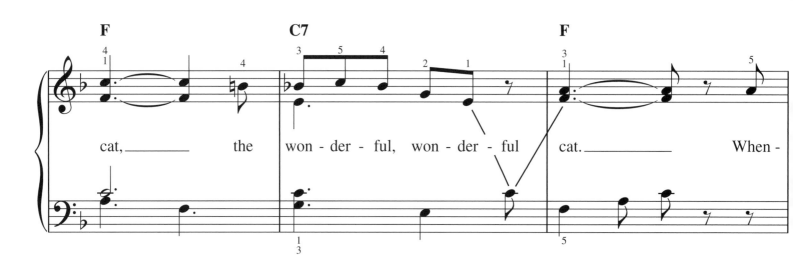

keeps you feel - ing mer - ry._____ Who? Fe - lix the

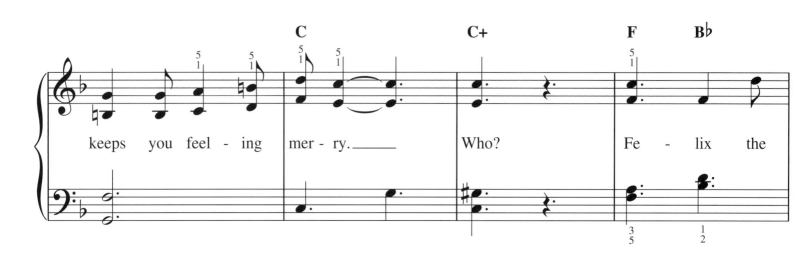

cat,_____ the won - der - ful, won - der - ful cat._____ When-

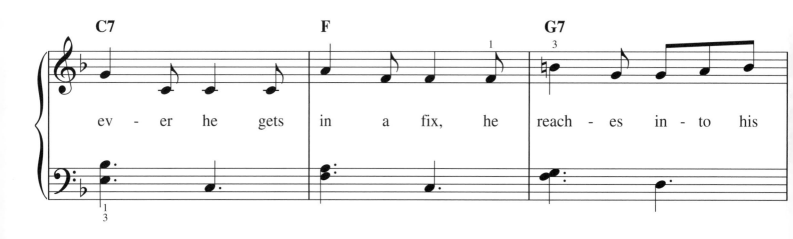

ev - er he gets in a fix, he reach - es in - to his

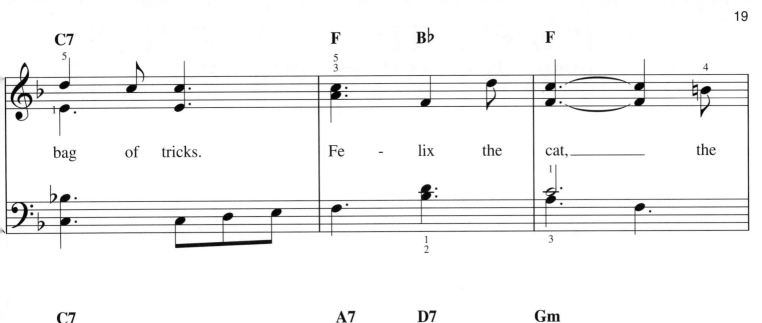

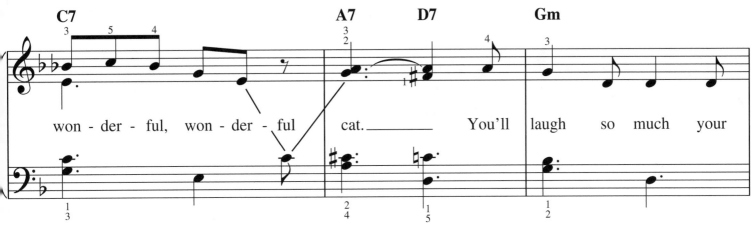

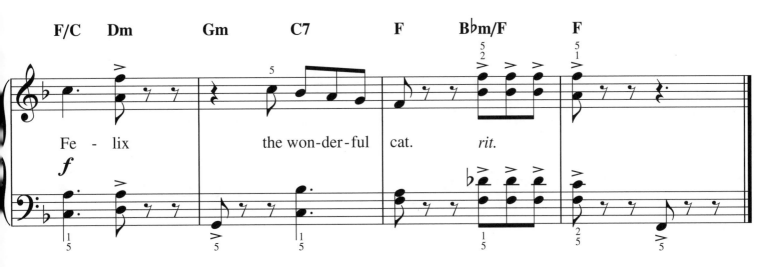

I'M POPEYE THE SAILOR MAN

Theme from the Paramount Cartoon POPEYE THE SAILOR

Words and Music by
SAMMY LERNER

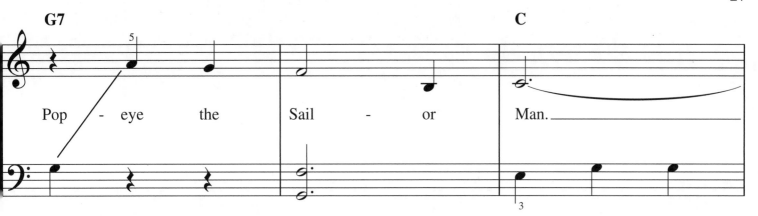

Pop - eye the Sail - or Man.

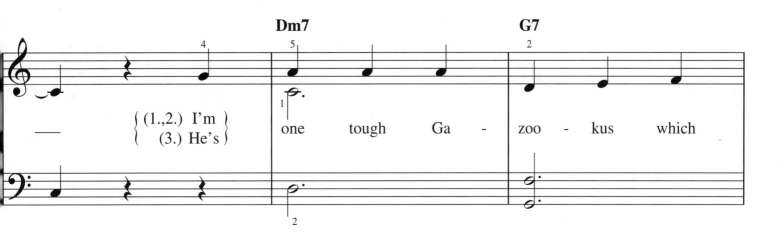

— { (1.,2.) I'm / (3.) He's } one tough Ga - zoo - kus which

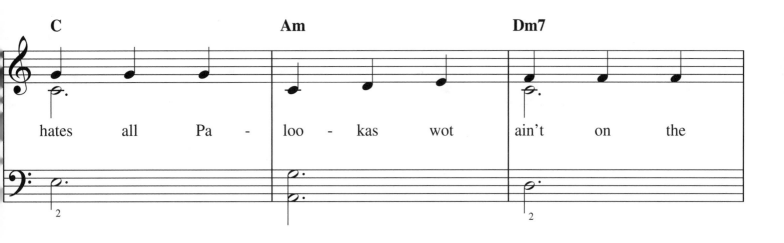

hates all Pa - loo - kas wot ain't on the

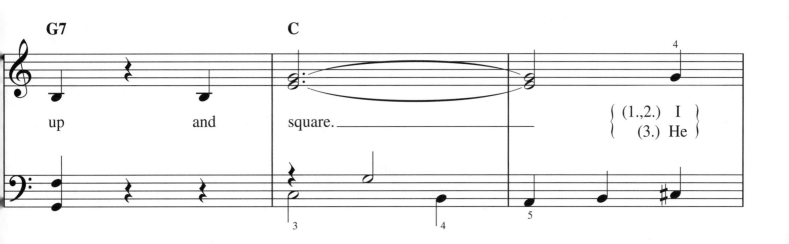

up and square. { (1.,2.) I / (3.) He }

22

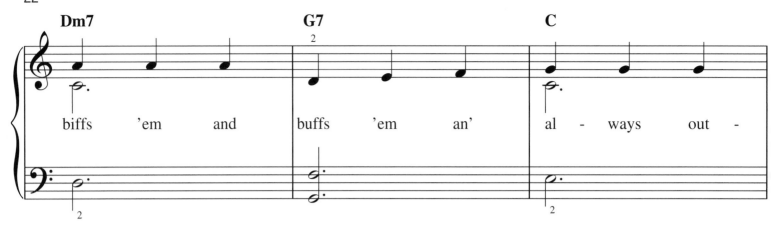

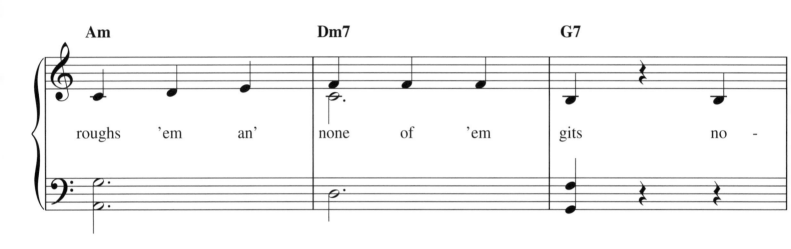

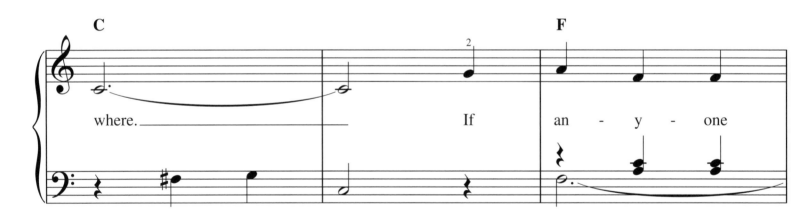

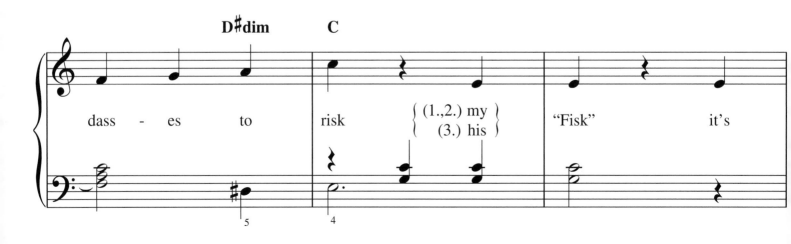

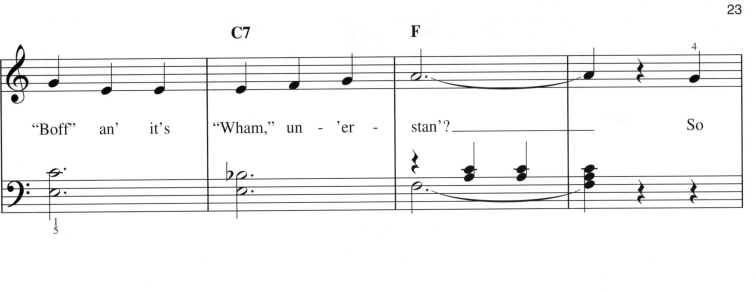

"Boff" an' it's "Wham," un - 'er - stan'? _____ So

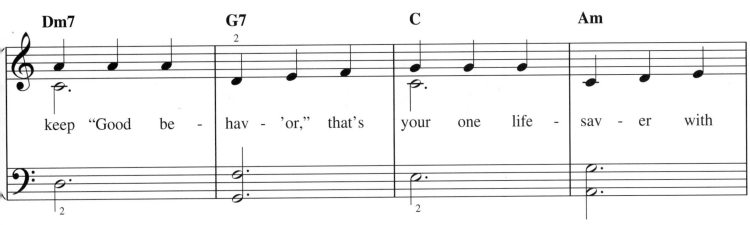

keep "Good be - hav - 'or," that's your one life - sav - er with

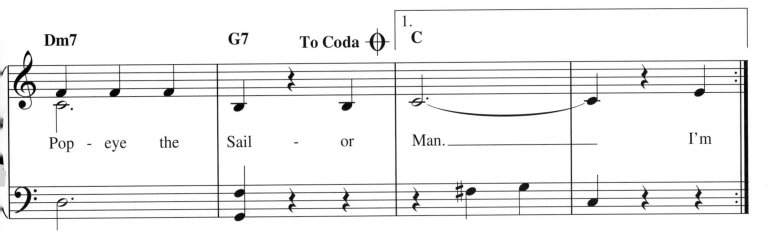

Pop - eye the Sail - or Man. _____ I'm

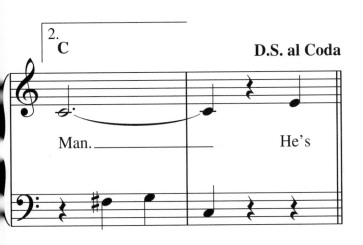

Man. _____ He's

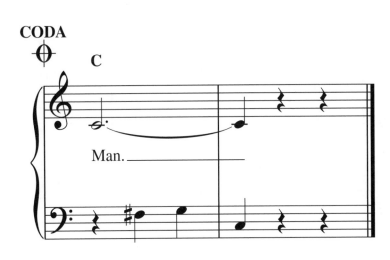

Man. _____

LINUS AND LUCY

By VINCE GUARALDI

MICKEY MOUSE MARCH

from Walt Disney's THE MICKEY MOUSE CLUB

Words and Music by
JIMMIE DODD

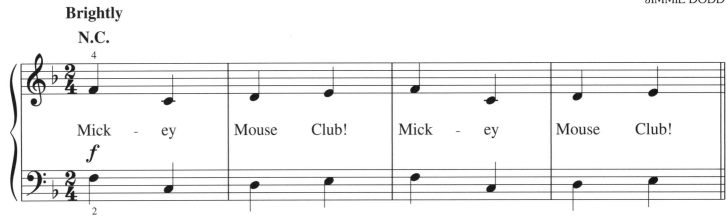

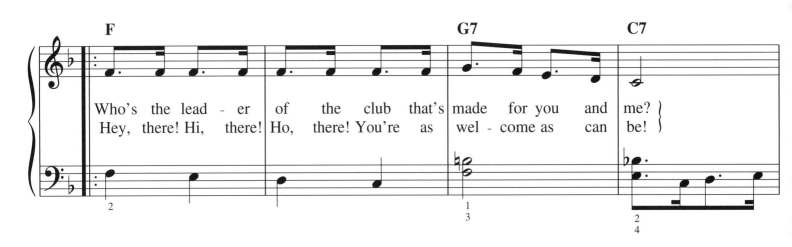

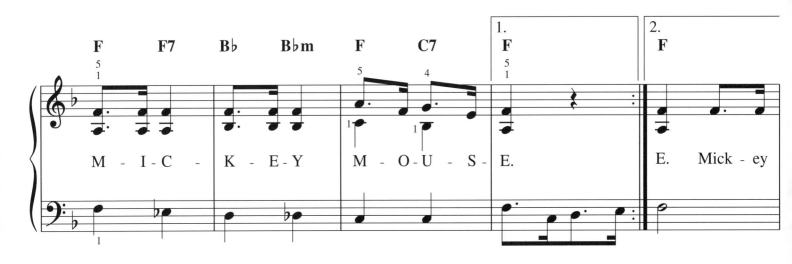

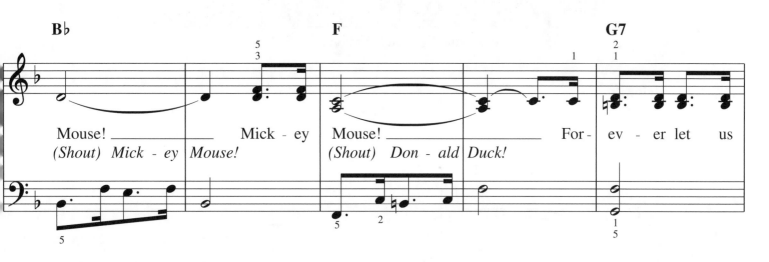

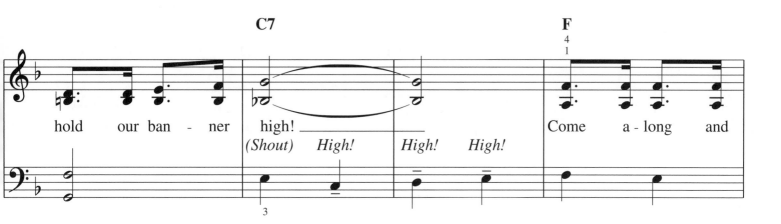

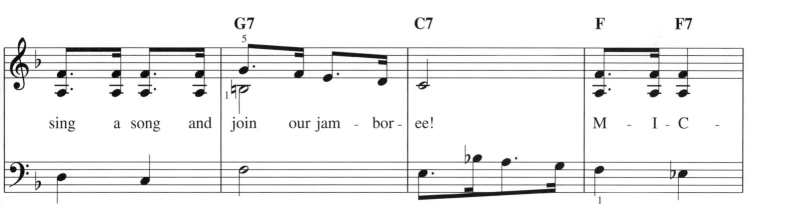

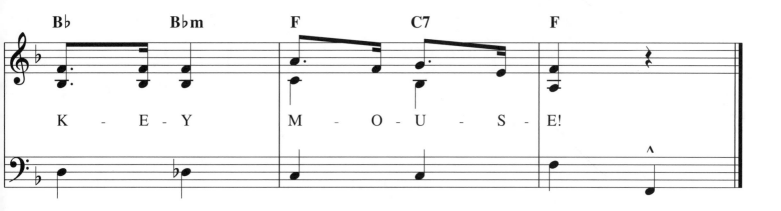

ROCKY & BULLWINKLE

from the Cartoon Television Series

By FRANK COMSTOCK

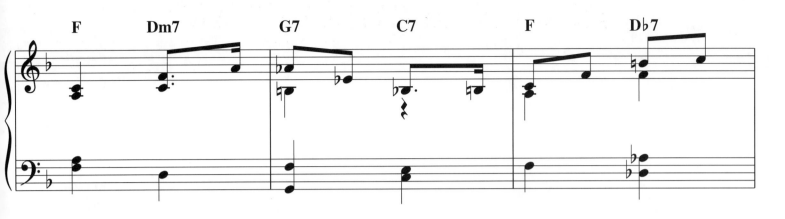

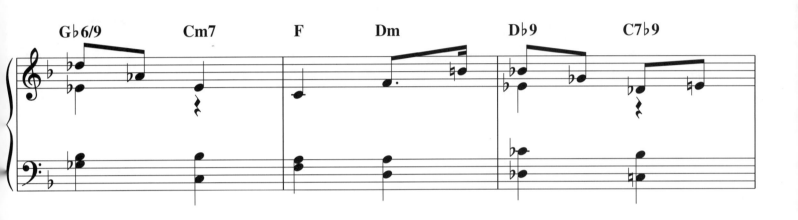

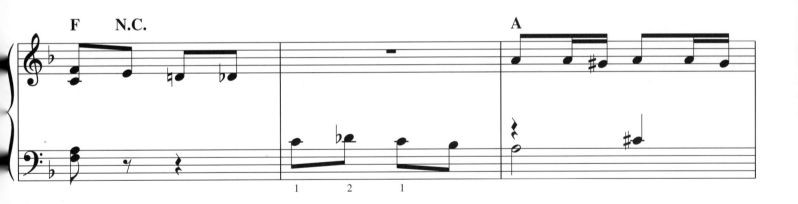

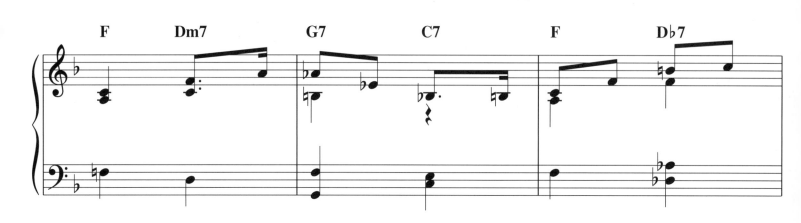

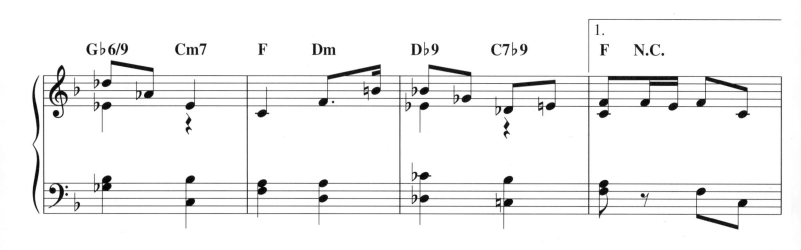

THEME FROM SPIDER MAN

Written by BOB HARRIS
and PAUL FRANCIS WEBSTER

Here comes the Spi - der - man.
There goes the Spi - der -

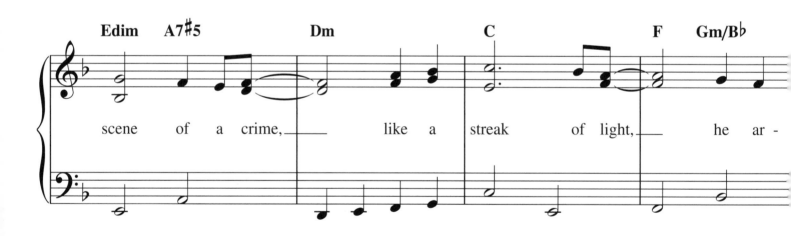

man. *mp* In the chill of night,___ at the

scene of a crime,___ like a streak of light,___ he ar -

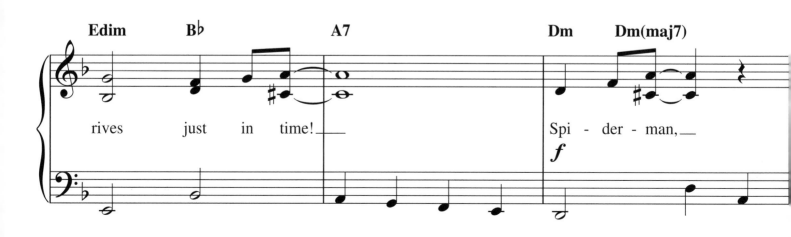

rives just in time!___ Spi - der - man,___

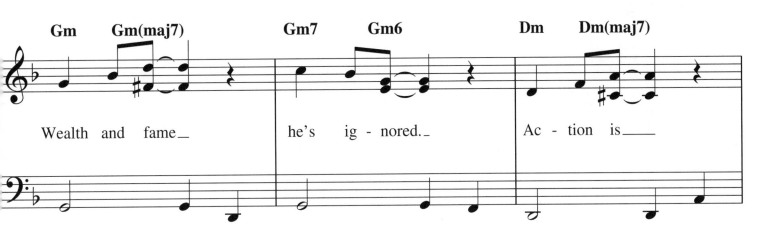

RUGRATS THEME

Words and Music by
MARK MOTHERSBAUGH

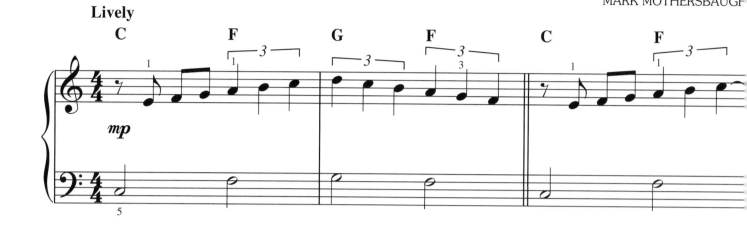

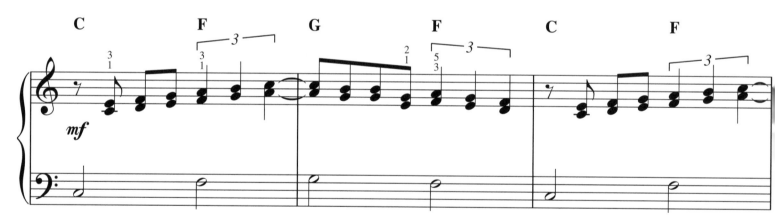

THEME FROM THE SIMPSONS™

from the Twentieth Century Fox Television Series THE SIMPSONS ™

Music by DANNY ELFMAN

Moderately fast, in 2

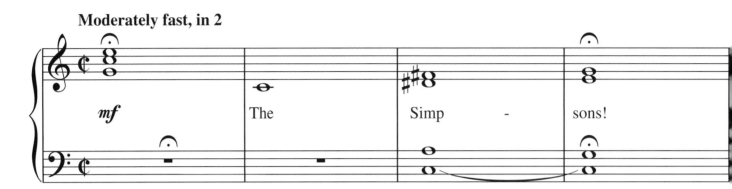

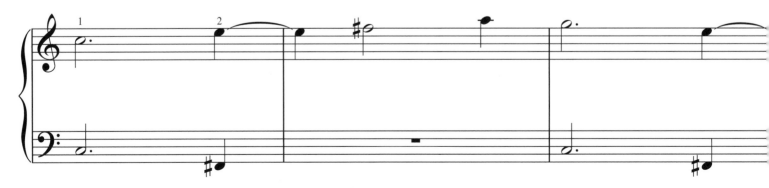

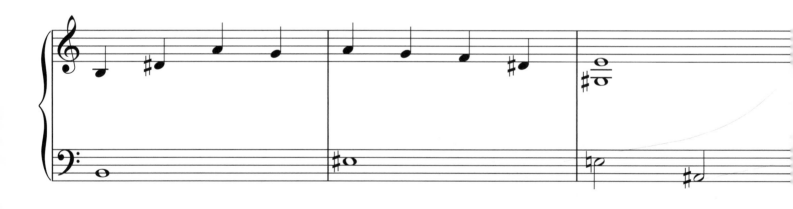

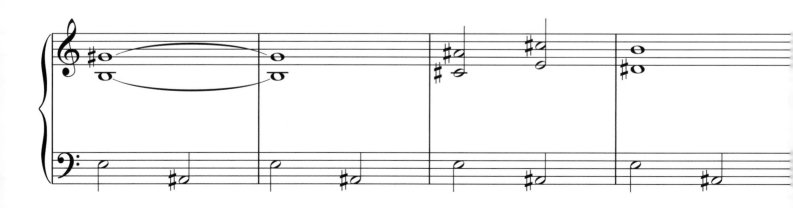

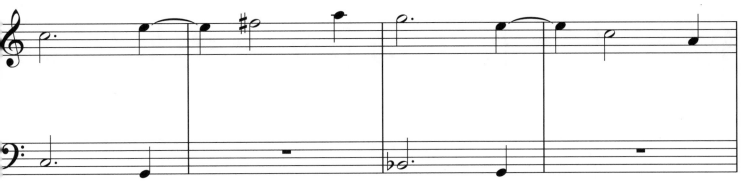

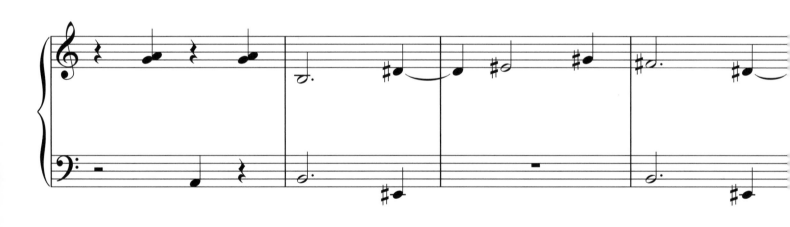

SPONGEBOB SQUAREPANTS THEME SONG

from SPONGEBOB SQUAREPANTS

Words and Music by MARK HARRISON
BLAISE SMITH, STEVE HILLENBURG
and DEREK DRYMON

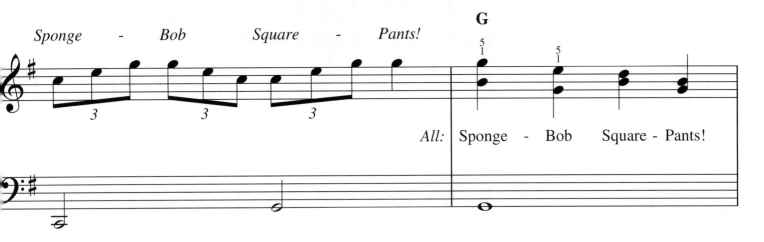

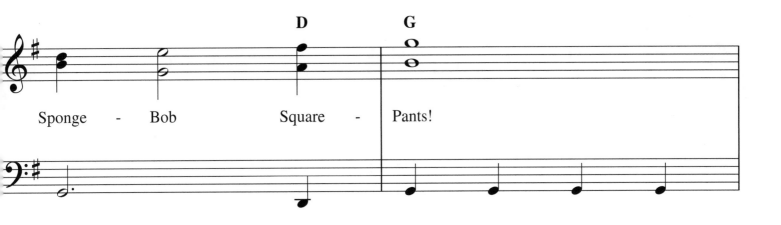

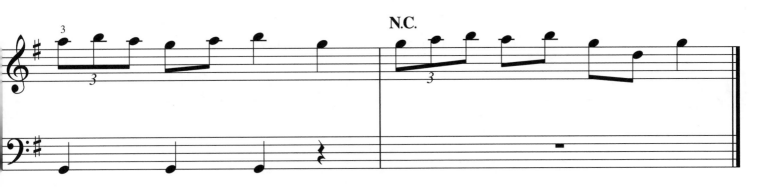

THIS IS IT
Theme from THE BUGS BUNNY SHOW

Words and Music by MACK DAVID
and JERRY LIVINGSTON

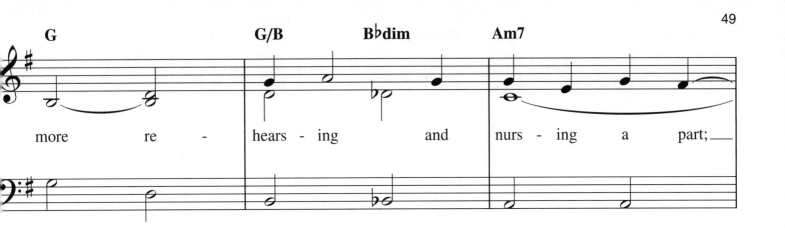

more re - hears - ing and nurs - ing a part;

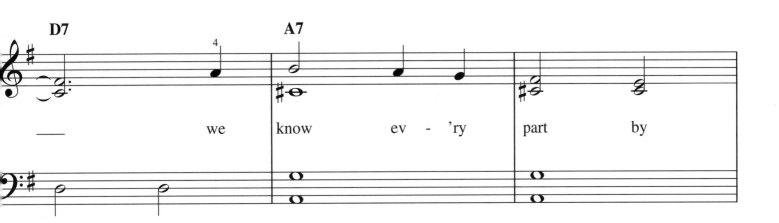

we know ev - 'ry part by

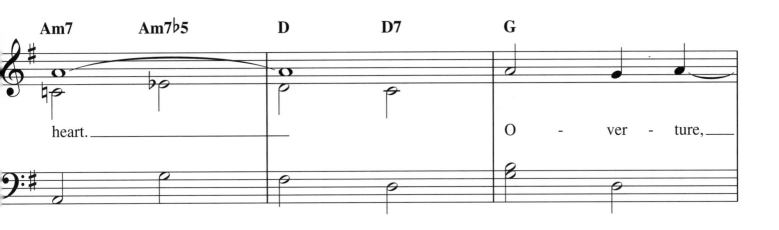

heart. O - ver - ture,

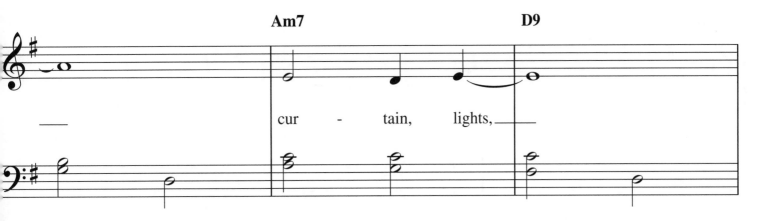

cur - tain, lights,

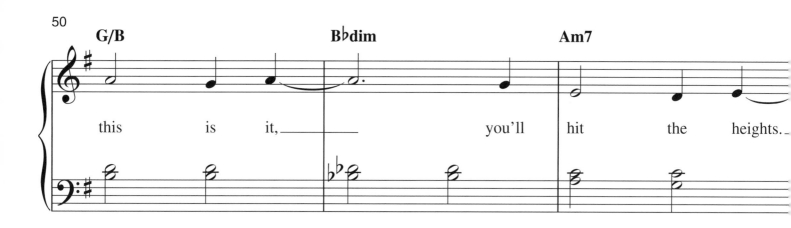

G/B **B♭dim** **Am7**

this is it,＿＿ you'll hit the heights.＿

D7 **G** **Em7**

＿ And oh, what heights we'll

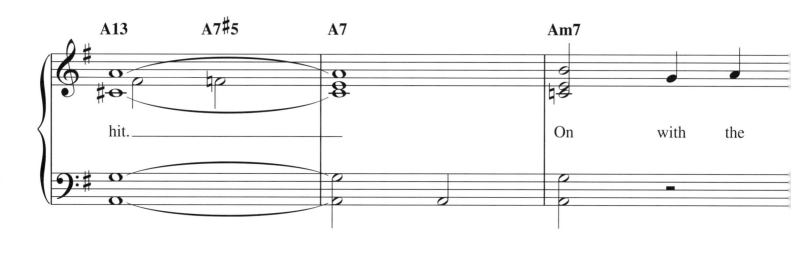

A13 **A7♯5** **A7** **Am7**

hit.＿＿ On with the

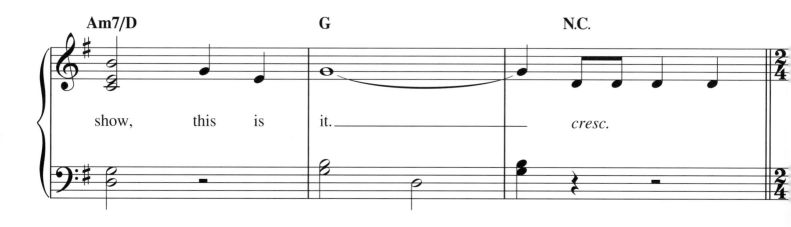

Am7/D **G** **N.C.**

show, this is it.＿＿ *cresc.*

March (♩ = ♪)

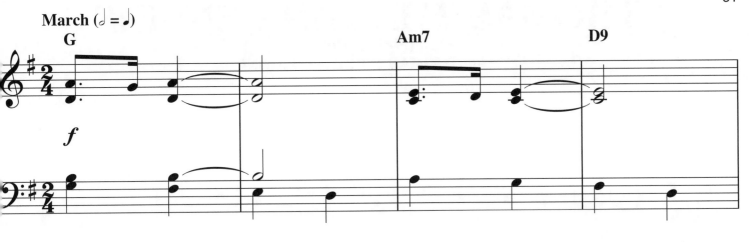

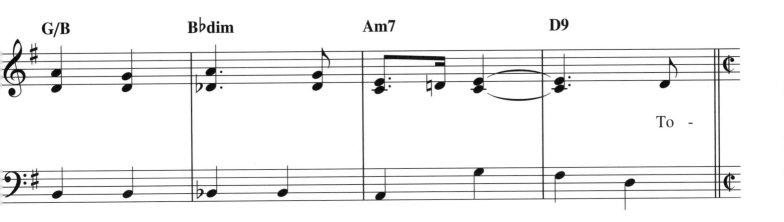

To -

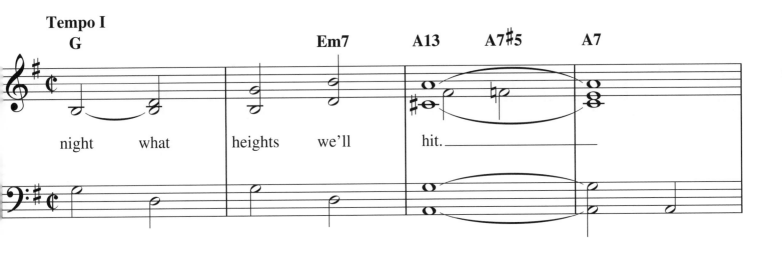

Tempo I

night   what   heights   we'll   hit.

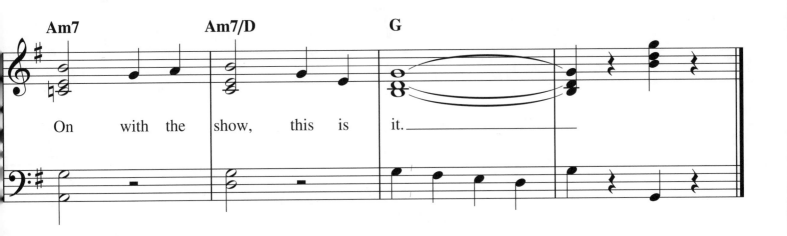

On   with the   show,   this is   it.

THOMAS THE TANK ENGINE
(Main Title)
from THOMAS THE TANK ENGINE

Words and Music by
ED WELCH

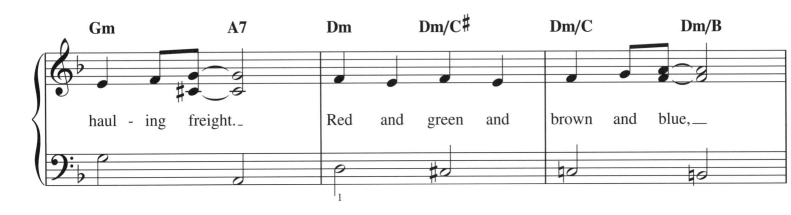

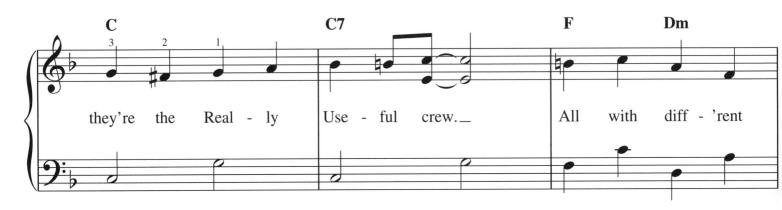

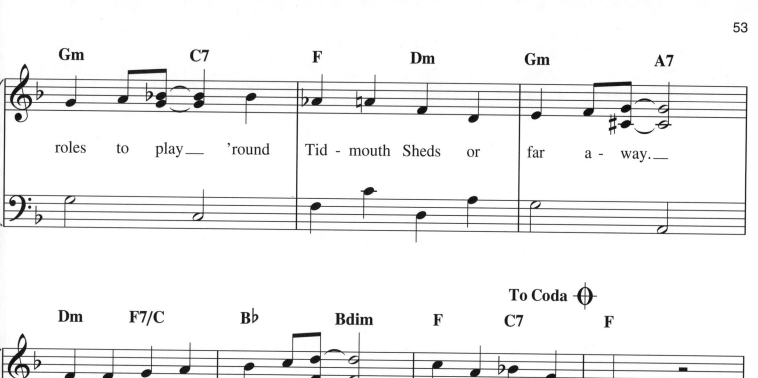

roles to play___ 'round Tid - mouth Sheds or far a - way.___

To Coda ⊕

Down the hills and 'round the bends,_ Thom - as and his friends.

James, he's vain but nev - er bad.___ Thom - as, he's the cheek - y lad.___

mp

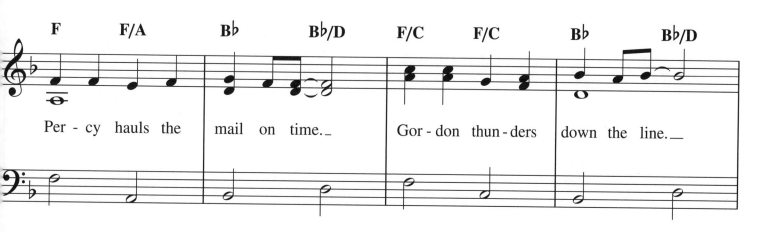

Per - cy hauls the mail on time._ Gor - don thun - ders down the line.___

Em - i - ly real - ly knows her stuff.__ Hen - ry toots and huffs and puffs.__

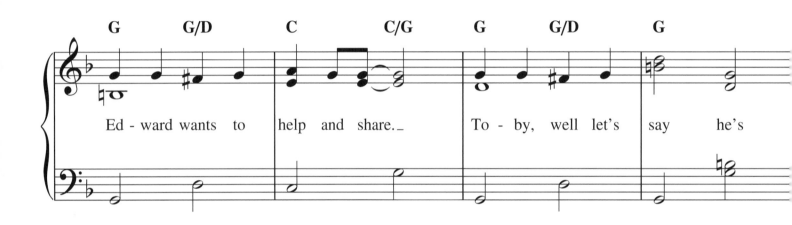

Ed - ward wants to help and share.__ To - by, well let's say he's

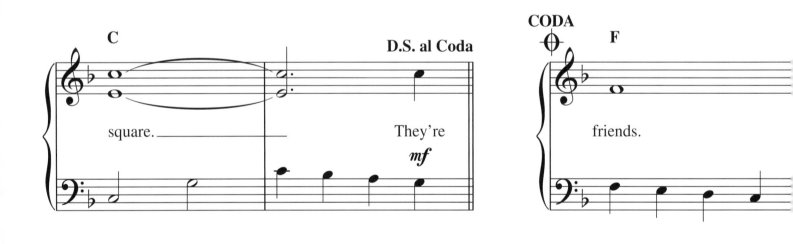

square.__ They're

D.S. al Coda

CODA

friends.

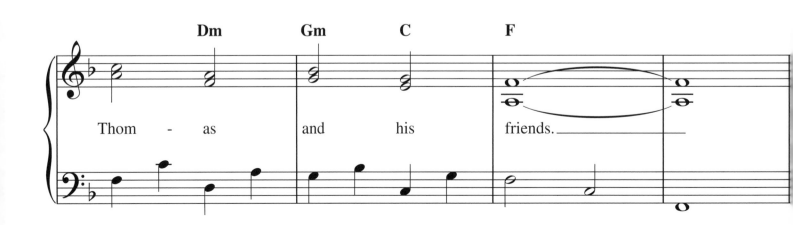

Thom - as and his friends.__

WINNIE THE POOH

from Walt Disney's THE MANY ADVENTURES OF WINNIE THE POOH

Words and Music by RICHARD M. SHERMAN
and ROBERT B. SHERMAN

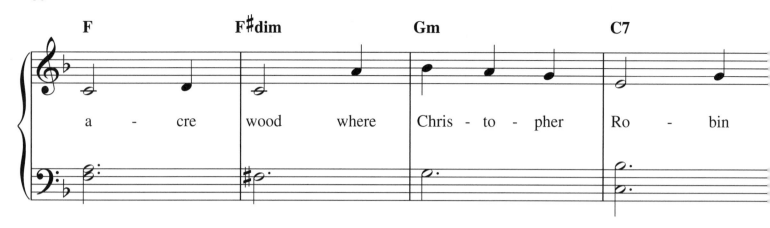

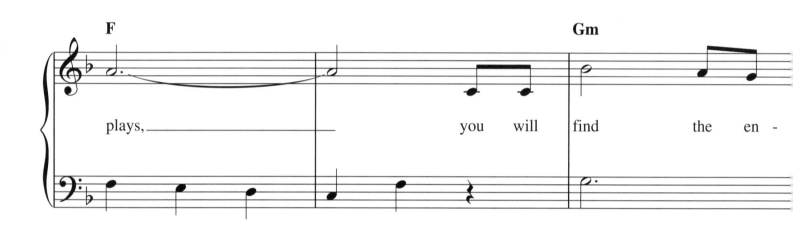

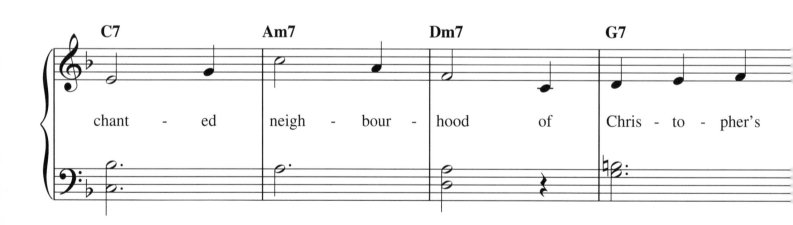

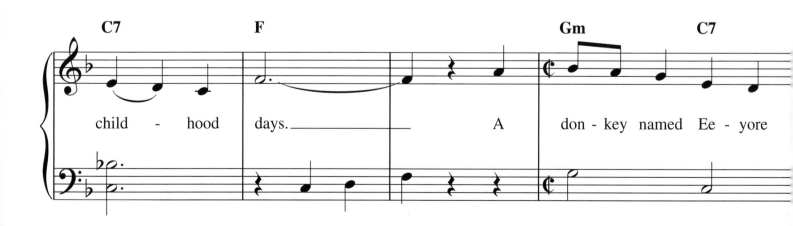

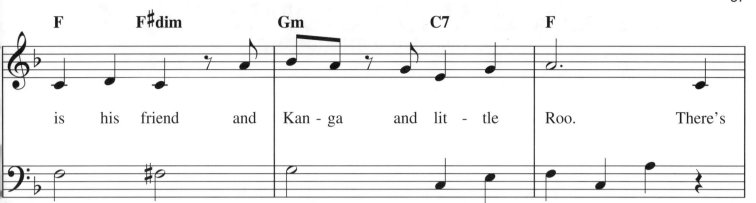

is his friend and Kan - ga and lit - tle Roo. There's

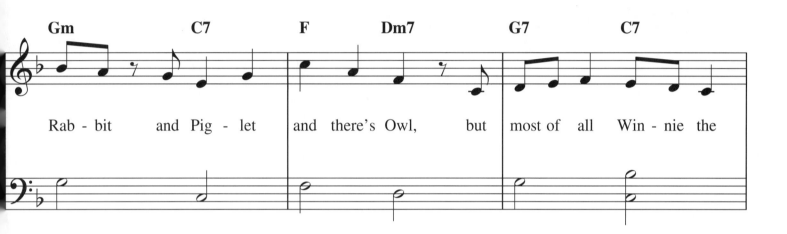

Rab - bit and Pig - let and there's Owl, but most of all Win - nie the

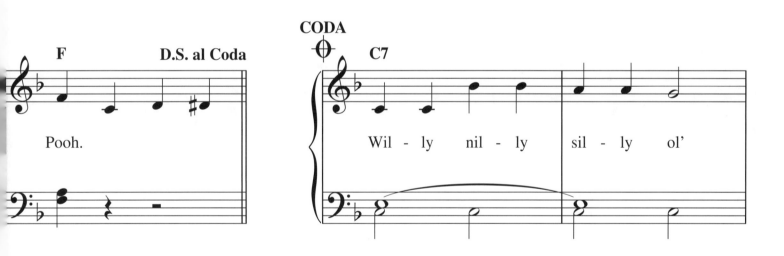

Pooh. Wil - ly nil - ly sil - ly ol'

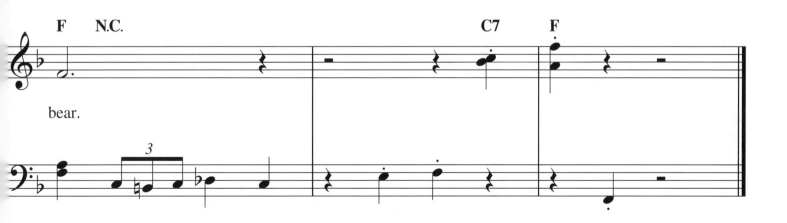

bear.

WALLACE AND GROMIT THEME
from WALLACE AND GROMIT

By JULIAN NOTT

WOODY WOODPECKER
from the Cartoon Television Series

Words and Music by GEORGE TIBBLES
and RAMEY IDRISS

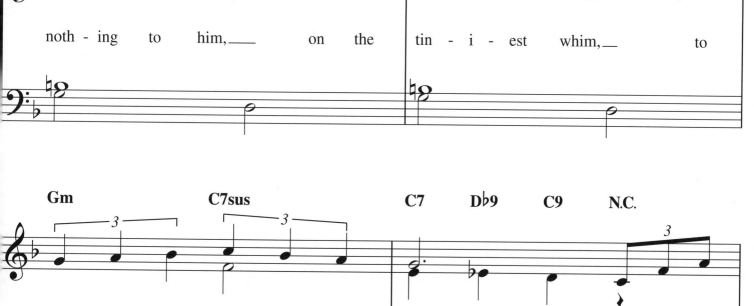

F   **Fmaj7**   **F#dim7**

ha   ha,   ha ha ha ha ha,   that's the

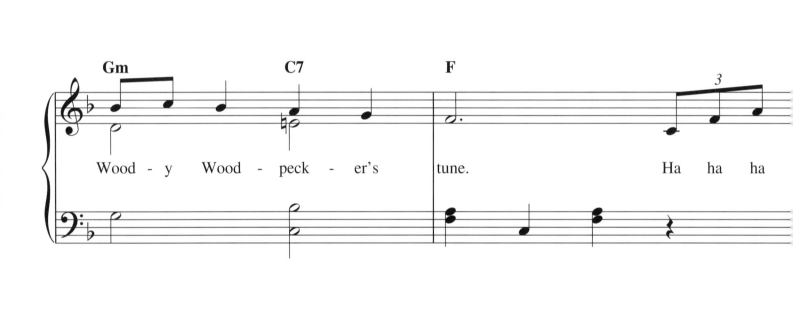

Gm   **C7**   **F**

Wood - y Wood - peck - er's   tune.   Ha ha ha

Fmaj7   **F#dim7**

ha   ha,   ha ha ha ha ha,   makes the

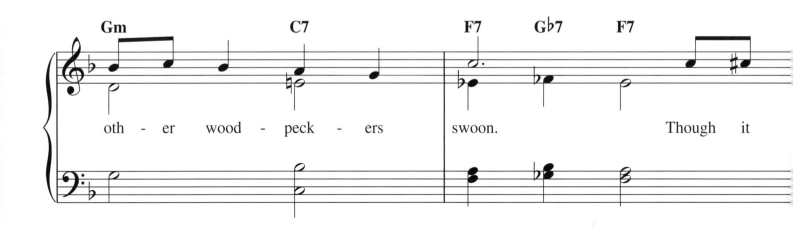

Gm   **C7**   **F7**   **G♭7**   **F7**

oth - er wood - peck - ers   swoon.   Though it

EASY PIANO CD PLAY-ALONGS
Orchestrated arrangements with you as the soloist!

This series lets you play along with great accompaniments to songs you know and love! Each book comes with a CD of complete professional performances and includes matching custom arrangements in Easy Piano format. With these books you can: Listen to complete professional performances of each of the songs; Play the Easy Piano arrangements along with the performances; Sing along with the recordings; Play the Easy Piano arrangements as solos, without the CD.

GREAT JAZZ STANDARDS – VOLUME 1
Bewitched • Do Nothin' Till You Hear from Me • Don't Get Around Much Anymore • How Deep Is the Ocean • I'm Beginning to See the Light • It Might As Well Be Spring • My Funny Valentine • Satin Doll • Stardust • That Old Black Magic.
00310916 Easy Piano $14.95

FAVORITE CLASSICAL THEMES – VOLUME 2
Bach: Air on the G String • Beethoven: Symphony No. 5, Excerpt • Bizet: Habanera • Franck: Panis Angelicus • Gounod: Ave Maria • Grieg: Morning • Handel: Hallelujah Chorus • Humperdinck: Evening Prayer • Mozart: Piano Concerto No. 21, Excerpt • Offenbach: Can Can • Pachelbel: Canon • Strauss: Emperor Waltz • Tchaikovsky: Waltz of the Flowers.
00310921 Easy Piano $14.95

BROADWAY FAVORITES – VOLUME 3
All I Ask of You • Beauty and the Beast • Bring Him Home • Cabaret • Close Every Door • I've Never Been in Love Before • If I Loved You • Memory • My Favorite Things • Some Enchanted Evening.
00310915 Easy Piano $14.95

ADULT CONTEMPORARY HITS – VOLUME 4
Amazed • Angel • Breathe • I Don't Want to Wait • I Hope You Dance • I Will Remember You • I'll Be • It's Your Love • The Power of Love • You'll Be in My Heart.
00310919 Easy Piano $14.95

HIT POP/ROCK BALLADS – VOLUME 5
Don't Let the Sun Go Down on Me • From a Distance • I Can't Make You Love Me • I'll Be There • Imagine • In My Room • My Heart Will Go On • Rainy Days and Mondays • Total Eclipse of the Heart • A Whiter Shade of Pale.
00310917 Easy Piano $14.95

Disney characters and artwork © Disney Enterprises, Inc.

Prices, contents and availability subject to change without notice.

LOVE SONG FAVORITES – VOLUME 6
Fields of Gold • I Honestly Love You • If • Lady in Red • More Than Words • Save the Best for Last • Three Times a Lady • Up Where We Belong • We've Only Just Begun • You Are So Beautiful.
00310918 Easy Piano $14.95

O HOLY NIGHT – VOLUME 7
Angels We Have Heard on High • Deck the Hall • Ding Dong! Merrily on High! • Go, Tell It on the Mountain • God Rest Ye Merry, Gentlemen • Good Christian Men, Rejoice • It Came upon the Midnight Clear • Jingle Bells • Lo, How a Rose E'er Blooming • O Come, All Ye Faithful • O Come, O Come Immanuel • O Holy Night • Once in Royal David's City • Silent Night • What Child Is This?
00310920 Easy Piano $14.95

A CHRISTIAN WEDDING – VOLUME 8
Cherish the Treasure • Commitment Song • How Beautiful • I Will Be Here • In This Very Room • The Lord's Prayer • Love Will Be Our Home • Parent's Prayer • This Is the Day • The Wedding.
00311104 Easy Piano $14.95

COUNTRY BALLADS – VOLUME 9
Always on My Mind • Could I Have This Dance • Crazy • Crying • Forever and Ever, Amen • He Stopped Loving Her Today • I Can Love You Like That • The Keeper of the Stars • Release Me • When You Say Nothing at All.
00311105 Easy Piano $14.95

MOVIE GREATS – VOLUME 10
And All That Jazz • Chariots of Fire • Come What May • Forrest Gump • I Finally Found Someone • Iris • Mission: Impossible Theme • Tears in Heaven • There You'll Be • A Wink and a Smile.
00311106 Easy Piano $14.95

DISNEY BLOCKBUSTERS – VOLUME 11
Be Our Guest • Can You Feel the Love Tonight • Go the Distance • Look Through My Eyes • Reflection • Two Worlds • Under the Sea • A Whole New World • Written in the Stars • You've Got a Friend in Me.
00311107 Easy Piano $14.95

CHRISTMAS FAVORITES – VOLUME 12
Blue Christmas • Frosty the Snow Man • Here Comes Santa Claus • A Holly Jolly Christmas • Home for the Holidays • I'll Be Home for Christmas • Merry Christmas, Darling • Mistletoe and Holly • Silver Bells • Wonderful Christmastime.
00311257 Easy Piano $14.95

CHILDREN'S SONGS – VOLUME 13
Any Dream Will Do • Do-Re-Mi • It's a Small World • Linus and Lucy • The Rainbow Connection • Splish Splash • This Land Is Your Land • Winnie the Pooh • Yellow Submarine • Zip-A-Dee-Doo-Dah.
00311258 Easy Piano $14.95

CHILDREN'S FAVORITES – VOLUME 14
Alphabet Song • Down by the Station • Eensy Weensy Spider • Frere Jacques • Home on the Range • I've Been Working on the Railroad • Kum Ba Yah • The Muffin Man • My Bonnie Lies over the Ocean • Oh Susanna • Old MacDonald • Row, Row, Row Your Boat • She'll Be Comin' 'Round the Mountain • This Old Man • Yankee Doodle.
00311259 Easy Piano $14.95

DISNEY'S BEST – VOLUME 15
Beauty and the Beast • Bibbidi-Bobbidi-Boo • Chim Chim Cher-ee • Colors of the Wind • Friend Like Me • Hakuna Matata • Part of Your World • Someday • When She Loved Me • You'll Be in My Heart.
00311260 Easy Piano $14.95

LENNON & McCARTNEY HITS – VOLUME 16
Eleanor Rigby • Hey Jude • The Long and Winding Road • Love Me Do • Lucy in the Sky with Diamonds • Nowhere Man • Please Please Me • Sgt. Pepper's Lonely Hearts Club Band • Strawberry Fields Forever • Yesterday.
00311262 Easy Piano $14.95

FOR MORE INFORMATION, SEE YOUR LOCAL MUSIC DEALER, OR WRITE TO:

HAL•LEONARD®
CORPORATION
7777 W. BLUEMOUND RD. P.O. BOX 13819 MILWAUKEE, WI 53213

www.halleonard.com

0200